Written by Bernard Planche
Illustrated by Donald Grant

Specialist Advisers:
Pierre and Bernadette Robbe,
Ethnologists, Museum of Man

ISBN 0-944589-12-X
First U.S. Publication 1988 by
Young Discovery Library
217 Main St. • Ossining, NY 10562

YOUNG DISCOVERY LIBRARY

Living with
the Eskimos

In Greenland,
　　　　a land of ice and snow...

YOUNG DISCOVERY LIBRARY

This is Greenland, the biggest island in the world.

It is very cold there; it is in the Arctic, nearly at the North Pole.

The people who live here are Eskimos.

They call themselves Inuit, which means 'the real people'. They live on the shores of the island, which are nearly always covered in snow. No one lives inland: it is a huge ice cap. In winter the sun

A 'real person'

hardly ever rises. There are places where it does not rise at all for months, and the night lasts for weeks on end.

Icebergs are huge lumps of ice which have fallen off glaciers into the sea. Most of an iceberg is underwater.

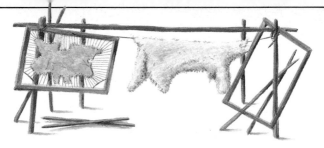

Polar bear and sealskins drying out of doors.

Eskimos live mainly by hunting and fishing, as it is too cold to grow any fruit or vegetables in the frozen ground. The villages are small, because there are not many people living in these cold places. The gaily painted houses brighten up the white landscape. Nowadays, almost all the villages have electricity. Fish are dried and kept outside in

the icy air. Kayaks and sleds are laid across frames so that the dogs won't chew the leather. There are almost twice as many dogs as there are people in the village!

The evenings are very long in winter.

In the warmth of the stove, which serves for both heating and cooking, the women tan hides while the men make harpoons. The children here are playing, trying to thread a needle through the holes in a piece of bone swinging from a cord.

Little figures carved by hand from sperm whale teeth.

What do Eskimos eat?

They eat meat or fish, either dried or boiled, seal blubber, and rice. Their water comes from ice which is melted in a bucket. In early times the walls of their huts were covered in sealskins to keep in the warmth. Not so long ago they were covered in newspapers — just as good at keeping in the heat, and much easier to catch! Nowadays, their walls are papered and painted just like ours are.

An Eskimo toy

How do the Eskimos keep out the cold?

Putting on two pairs of boots, trousers made of bearskin, and a hooded jacket made of sealskin or caribou hide, they go out even when it's -50°F. It never gets as cold as that for us!

The women chew on the leather to make it soft enough to sew.

The kind of clothes worn particularly in Thule, in northern Greenland.

12

For special occasions, the women wear red jackets with a cape on top. The capes are decorated all over with glass beads. The women spend a lot of time and imagination working out the prettiest designs. They also wear decorated boots. The young women wear white boots, while the older women wear red ones.

Scraper, or ulu, for cleaning hides.

A shop right in the north of Greenland, selling every sort of tool and supply. Nowadays a lot of the goods are delivered by helicopter.

Huskies

Eskimos use dogs to pull their sleds when they go out hunting or fishing. A team of dogs works together pulling a sled, with the most intelligent and bravest dog in front as leader. The dogs are harnessed in a fan shape, each in its special place. The master gives his orders to the leader.

The leader is often a female, while the other dogs may be her grown-up puppies.

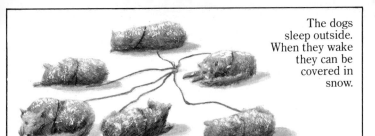

The dogs sleep outside. When they wake they can be covered in snow.

Their thick fur protects them from the cold as they lie curled up in the snow, their noses tucked under their tails. When they get up, they have to crack their way out of their snow shells. They are strong and tireless, and they can pull very heavy loads. A hunter setting out on an expedition needs to pack all sorts of things: a gun, an axe, a harpoon, a saw, a fur rug, a tent, a cooking stove and saucepan, food...

To make the dogs turn right, their master will shout "illi-illi", and "ka-ka" to make them go left.

When they go downhill, the dogs are tied behind the sled to stop it from going too fast.

19

How to go shark fishing
Shark fishing used to be much more common than it is now. The fisherman would make a hole in the ice, and wait.

When the shark took the bait, it was pulled out of the water, where it immediately froze in the cold air. Dried shark meat was used for dog food.

Inside an igloo
seen from
on top.

In the north of Greenland, when the hunters are too far from the village to return in the evening, they build themselves a shelter in the snow: an **igloo.** Using a saw, they cut out big blocks of hard snow. In earlier times, they used a bone knife to cut the snow.

When the blocks are cut, they are piled like bricks on top of each other, in a spiral shape like a snail's shell. The hardened blocks make a shelter from the wind and cold. The light gets through the ice, and inside the igloo it is bright and cheerful. A small hole in the roof lets out the fumes from the cookstove.

Inside an igloo seen
from the side. Benches to
sit on are cut from the
hard snow.

Musk oxen

Animals in the cold: the arctic fox (1) and the polar bear (2) hunt on the ice pack. When winter approaches, the wolf (3) and the caribou (4) take shelter on the grassy plains to the south. Polar waters are full of tiny plants and animals which attract whales (5). Seals (6) and walrus feed on the fish which live in the icy seas.

Pipe carved from a walrus tusk

The walrus rakes the seabed with its tusks to find shellfish.

25

Polar bears sleep on the ice

Well protected by a layer of blubber under their skin and by their thick fur, polar bears live all their lives on the ice. They are good swimmers, even in the icy cold water, and will eat hundreds of pounds of fish in a single meal!

Their white fur makes them almost invisible against the white snow, so that they can sneak up on their prey. They sometimes catch seals as they lie and bask on the ice.

A polar bear mother and her young in their den. A female bear can have young every two years. When they're born, the cubs are as small as rabbits.

Seals are very good at swimming.
They aren't fish, though — they are marine mammals. They have to come up to the surface to breathe. When the sea is frozen, they make air holes in the ice. In summer, they like to lie and bask in the sunshine. Then the Eskimos hunt them, lying behind

Seal pups are at least a month old before they have their first swim in the sea; before that their fur is not waterproof.

white screens which are supported on little skis. Only the hunter's gun pokes through as he creeps up on the seals,

slowly and silently.
He must go very carefully, not to frighten the seals away.

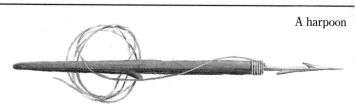

A harpoon

Seals are very precious to the Eskimos.

They provide meat, blubber, oil, skin for clothing, bones for toys and tools, and tendons which are used as thread for sewing.

Hunting by kayak: Eskimo canoes covered in sealskins, are called kayaks. There is room for just one person. He slides into the kayak through a tight-fitting hole in the top. The kayak is steered by a double-ended paddle, and can turn right over in the water without sinking — the hunter is safe, just very cold and wet!

When spring returns, the sun climbs higher and higher in the sky, until, for a few weeks in midsummer, it doesn't set at all!

The sea is no longer locked in ice. Boats begin to arrive bringing fresh fruit and vegetables!

The birds return to the coast in such numbers that you can sit and catch them with a net.

Eider duck

At the end of the summer, Eskimos collect bilberries and crowberries. But the warm season doesn't last long; it's all over in three months.

In Canada, snowmobiles are often used instead of dogs to pull sleds

The Inuit live in other countries too:
some live in northern Canada, others in Alaska, or in Siberia, a region in the north of the USSR. They don't all speak exactly the same language, but they can usually understand each other.

Other people of the snows
Tribes of Indians, such as the Hurons and the Iroquois, live in the huge forests in northern Canada. In the north of Europe, there lives a very special people called the Lapps.

A Lapp in his traditional red and blue clothes riding on a sled pulled by a reindeer.

A settlement built of logs in the Canadian forest

Laplanders

The Lapps live right up in the north of Finland, Norway and Sweden, crossing over from country to country as they follow the herds of reindeer. The Lapps depend on reindeer for food and clothing, and have to move with the herds as they find fresh grass and moss to eat.

A truck with caterpillar tracks

Lapps are the last real nomads in Europe, moving from place to place instead of having one settled home to live in.

Indian sled in the Canadian forest

Index

The Kayak

Over the briny wave I go,
In spite of the weather, in spite of the snow:
What cares the hardy Eskimo?
In my little skiff, with paddle and lance,
I glide where the foaming billows dance.

Round me the seabirds slip and soar;
Like me, they love the ocean's roar.
Sometimes a floating iceberg gleams
Above me with its melting streams;
Sometimes a rushing wave will fall
Down on my skiff and cover it all

But what care I for a wave's attack?
With my paddle I right my little kayak,
And then its weight I speedily trim,
And over the water away I skim.